Ways to Go

CARS GO!

By John Matthew Williams

Gareth Stevens
PUBLISHING

Please visit our website, www.garethstevens.com. For a free color catalog of all our high-quality books, call toll free 1-800-542-2595 or fax 1-877-542-2596.

Cataloging-in-Publication Data
Names: Williams, John Matthew.
Title: Cars go! / John Matthew Williams.
Description: New York : Gareth Stevens Publishing, 2018. | Series: Ways to go | Includes index.
Identifiers: ISBN 9781538210178 (pbk.) | ISBN 9781538210185 (library bound) | ISBN 9781538210222 (6 pack)
Subjects: LCSH: Automobiles–Juvenile literature.
Classification: LCC TL147.W55 2018 | DDC 629.222–dc23

First Edition

Published in 2018 by
Gareth Stevens Publishing
111 East 14th Street, Suite 349
New York, NY 10003

Editor: Kate Mikoley
Designer: Sam DeMartin

Photo credits: Cover, p. 1 Mino Surkala/Shutterstock.com; p. 5 TTstudio/Shutterstock.com; p. 7 photo-denver/Shutterstock.com; pp. 9, 24 (steering wheel) Andrey_Popov/Shutterstock.com; pp. 11, 24 (pedal) kryzhov/Shutterstock.com; p. 13 © JackJelly/istockphoto.com; p. 15 Nina Raingold/Getty Images News/Getty Images; p. 17 (both) alice-photo/Shutterstock.com; p. 19 Solomia Malovana/Shutterstock.com; p. 21 bonzodog/Shutterstock.com; p. 23 Melpomene/Shutterstock.com; p. 24 (wheel) Zavatskiy Aleksandr/Shutterstock.com.

Printed in the United States of America

CPSIA compliance information: Batch #CW18GS: For further information contact Gareth Stevens, New York, New York at 1-800-542-2595.

Contents

Cars help us go all around!

They have four wheels.

The steering wheel helps cars turn.

Cars have two pedals. People push them with their feet.

One pedal makes
the car go.
The other makes it stop.

STOP

People drive cars on streets and roads.

Red lights mean stop.
Green lights mean go.

Cars can take you
to the store.
They can also take you
on trips.

Some cars go very fast.

Cities have lots of cars.

Words to Know

steering wheel

pedal

wheel

Index